Woodrow Wilson

Woodrow Wilson

Barbara Silberdick Feinberg

AMERICA'S

28TH

PRESIDENT

Children's Press®
A Division of Scholastic Inc.
New York / Toronto / London / Auckland / Sydney
Mexico City / New Delhi / Hong Kong
Danbury, Connecticut

Library of Congress Cataloging-in-Publication Data

Feinberg, Barbara Silberdick.
    Woodrow Wilson / by Barbara Silberdick Feinberg.
        p. cm.—(Encyclopedia of presidents)
    Includes bibliographical references and index.
  ISBN 0-516-22968-0
    1. Wilson, Woodrow, 1856–1924—Juvenile literature. 2. Presidents—United
States—Biography—Juvenile literature. [1. Wilson, Woodrow, 1856–1924.
2. Presidents.] I. Title. II. Encyclopedia of presidents. Second series.
E767.F45 2004
973.91'3'092—dc22   2003027243

CHILDREN'S PRESS and associated logos are trademarks and or registered
trademarks of Scholastic Library Publishing. SCHOLASTIC and associated
logos are trademarks and or registered trademarks of Scholastic Inc.
1 2 3 4 5 6 7 8 9 10 R 13 12 11 10 09 08 07 06 05 04

Contents

Chapter 1

A Controversial President ————————

When Woodrow Wilson became the 28th president of the United States in 1912, he was the first professional scholar and college teacher ever elected. As president of Princeton University, he had achieved educational reforms that made it one of America's most admired institutions of learning. As governor of New Jersey, he had brought political reforms to the state's government.

As president, Wilson continued his reforming ways, helping pass legislation that modernized the federal government and extended its power. During his second term, he led the United States into the Great War (now known as World War I), sending millions of American troops to fight in Europe. At war's end, he personally helped draft the peace treaty, urging the countries of the world to form the League of Nations, an international organization to settle international conflicts. In the end, the president failed to persuade his own country to participate in the new organization, and he left office a defeated man.

Wilson's successes and failures made him an important but controversial president. He brought high ideals and aspirations to the presidency, but his stubborn refusal to compromise finally helped defeat his most cherished dreams.

Early Years

Thomas Woodrow Wilson was born on December 28, 1856, in Staunton, Virginia. His father, Joseph Ruggles Wilson, was a Presbyterian minister who met and married Jessie Woodrow in Ohio. The couple settled in the South in 1851, and when Thomas Woodrow was born, they already had two daughters, Marion (born 1850) and Annie (born 1854). Nearly ten years later, a second son, Joseph, was born.

Before young Tommy turned two years old, the Wilson family moved to Augusta, Georgia, where his father became the pastor of a Presbyterian congregation. Wilson later recalled, "My earliest recollection is of standing at my father's gateway in Augusta, Georgia, when I was four years old, and hearing someone pass and say that Mr. Lincoln was elected and there was to be war." The U.S. Civil War began in 1861.

The war affected Tommy's life. His father served briefly as a chaplain in the Confederate army and preached that the Bible accepted slavery. Later,

Thomas Woodrow Wilson was born in this house in Staunton, Virginia, in 1856.

Tommy saw Union prisoners in a churchyard stockade, and wounded soldiers were treated in his father's church. Schools were closed, and so it was hard for Tommy to learn or to make friends. His family became a source of education and companionship for him. The Wilsons started each day with a Bible reading, prayer, and hymns. As the baby of the family, Tommy was coddled by his mother and adoring sisters.

Each week, father and son walked around town, studying the city's mills and warehouses. His father asked Tommy questions about what they had seen and required that he reply in carefully formed sentences. He taught Tommy the importance of choosing words that precisely expressed his ideas. His son later called Reverend Wilson "one of the most inspiring fathers that a lad was ever blessed with."

Wilson's parents, Joseph Ruggles Wilson and Jessie Woodrow Wilson.

The Schoolboy

At the end of the war, schools reopened, and Tommy attended an academy run by former Confederate officer Joseph T. Derry. He was not a good student, but he began to make friends his own age. They formed a baseball team, the Light Foots, whose members met in the Wilsons' barn. Tommy drew up its rules of organization and behavior. Perhaps he learned something about the rules of parliamentary procedure from listening at Presbyterian church meetings. Tommy also enjoyed novels about colonial America. He acted out their plots with his cousins.

In 1870, when Tommy was 14, the Wilsons moved to Columbia, South Carolina. His father became a professor at a theological seminary, a college to train Presbyterian ministers. The move brought the Wilsons closer to uncles,

Did Tommy Have Dyslexia?

Dyslexia is a learning disorder that affects the ability to read and write. This disability was not recognized during Wilson's lifetime, but he had many of the symptoms. He did not recognize alphabet letters until he was about nine years old. He could not read easily until he was about eleven or twelve. His teachers believed he was a lazy student, but the real cause of his difficulty may have been dyslexia, in which a reader has trouble seeing letters in their proper order.

☆ ★ ☆

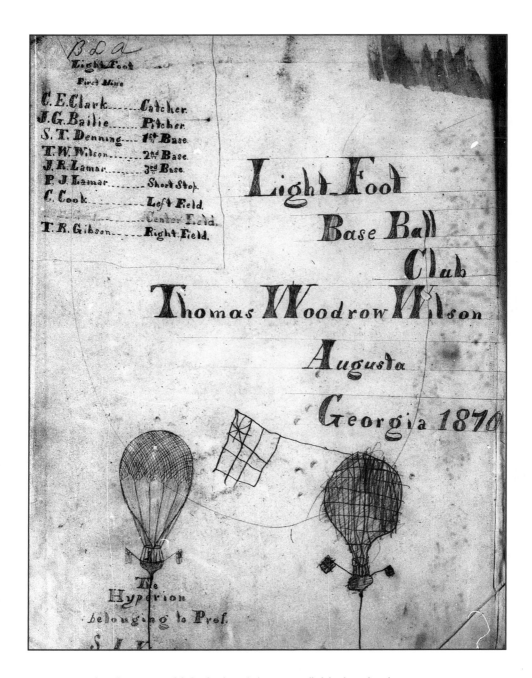

Young Tommy Wilson drew up a careful plan for the Light Foot Base Ball Club. This is the title page.

The Wilson home in Columbia, South Carolina, where Wilson spent his teenage years.

cousins, and other family members who lived near the city. In addition, Professor

Wilson was able to plan and build a new house for his family.

Tommy was enrolled in private school, but he soon grew bored with

Greek and Latin, and his grades fell. He began to sit in on classes at the seminary.

About this time he found a magazine advertisement for a course that would teach

him shorthand, a quick way of writing that used abbreviations for common words and sounds. He sent away for the course and soon learned to write in shorthand, a skill he used for the rest of his life. At about the same time, Wilson also developed a passion for ships and naval warfare, filling his notebooks with drawings of vessels on imaginary missions. "I led a dream life," he wrote later.

When he was 17, Tommy Wilson applied for formal membership in the Presbyterian Church. His religious beliefs would provide a strong support throughout his life. He later said, "My life would not be worth living if it were not for the driving power of religion." He gradually decided, however, that he would not become a Presbyterian minister like his father, but devote his life to more worldly concerns.

College Years

In the fall of 1873, Wilson left home for the first time to attend Davidson College in North Carolina. Davidson was supported by the Presbyterian Church, and many of its students were preparing for the ministry. Tommy achieved good grades and joined the debating society, but after a year of study, he withdrew from the school. Still only 17 years old, he may have been homesick, or he may have been encouraged to return home by his family.

In 1874 the family moved to Wilmington, North Carolina, near the Atlantic Ocean. Wilson's father again became pastor of a church. For the next year, young Wilson pursued his interest in ships. He often walked along the town's waterfront, watching the boats and talking to sailors. He dreamed of a career in the navy, but his mother made him promise not to expose himself to the dangers of a military life.

He also continued to study on his own, and in the fall of 1875, he enrolled at the College of New Jersey at Princeton. Founded in 1746, the school was supported by the Presbyterian Church and had about 500 students. Wilson found that the college was not as focused on religious concerns as Davidson had been. It attracted the sons of wealthy and socially important families, and only a few students were preparing for the ministry.

For the next three years, Wilson lived in a dormitory, and joined the Alligators, an eating club. Eating clubs had been set up because the college did not have facilities to feed all of its students. They gradually had become social clubs

Wilson during his student days at Princeton.

resembling today's fraternities. Members of the same club often made friendships that lasted a lifetime.

Once again, Wilson was soon bored by his studies. Talking with his friends proved more interesting than any of his classes. He helped form an organization called the Liberal Debating Club, where members could express their views and sharpen their speaking skills. They turned the club into a model of the British *Parliament*, the lawmaking body of British government. Wilson was elected prime minister, or parliamentary leader and government spokesman. The idea of a government answerable to the wishes of a majority led Wilson to admire Britain's system of government.

Studying in a northern college also changed Wilson's view of recent U.S. history. He had grown up an ardent supporter of the South in the Civil War, but he gradually realized that its cause included continuing slavery, which he could not defend. He continued to favor segregation of the races, however, and had a low opinion of the abilities of African Americans.

In 1876, Wilson got caught up in campus arguments over the presidential election. In November, Republican Rutherford B. Hayes and Democrat Samuel J. Tilden ran such a close race that neither could claim victory in the election. Tilden had more popular votes, but was one short of a majority in the *electoral college* (the body made up of state representatives that officially elects a president).

Republicans and Democrats at Princeton demonstrated, fought, and made stirring speeches for their candidates. Wilson wrote in his diary, "I did no studying in the evening and went to bed . . . tired out with shouting and excitement." He favored Tilden, the Democrat, but in the end, Hayes was declared president by a special electoral commission set up by Congress. Wilson saw the result as an argument against the power and the corrupt nature of Congress.

Wilson (holding his hat at right) was a member of the Alligator Eating Club. Later, as president of Princeton, he tried to abolish eating clubs.

Wilson became a pioneering staff member of the *Princetonian*, the college newspaper, which was first published in 1876. As managing editor, he dealt with the paper's business matters and also wrote many of its articles. He also helped coach the college football team and saw that its exploits were covered in the *Princetonian*.

In the spring of 1879, Wilson graduated 38th in a class of 107, with an average of 90.3. By this time he was certain that he was not cut out to be a minister. Perhaps studying law would let him use the public speaking skills he had begun to discover at Princeton.

Chapter 2

A Lawyer

The fall after his college graduation, Wilson entered the University of Virginia Law School. He hoped that becoming a lawyer would lead to a career in politics. He soon came to regret his decision. He found that studying legal statutes and procedures was tiresome. During his stay at Virginia, he decided to use his middle name, asking people to call him Woodrow instead of Tommy. Woodrow was his mother's maiden name, and his mother may have encouraged him to make the change.

Halfway through his second year, Wilson gave up his studies. He was bored, and he may have been ill as well. He returned to the family home in Wilmington. There he taught Latin to his brother Joseph, and continued to study law by himself. He was also trying to work out his future. "I make frequent extemporaneous addresses to the empty benches in my father's church in order to get a mastery of easy and correct and elegant expression, in preparation for the future," he wrote to a friend.

In 1882, Wilson went into partnership with a former classmate at Virginia to practice law in Atlanta, Georgia. He found that he could not stand the drudgery of a day-to-day legal practice. He remained interested in the principles of the law but disliked the petty quarrels and broken promises that lay behind most of the cases.

A Man in Love

While he was working in Atlanta, Wilson traveled to Rome, Georgia, on a family legal matter. At a church service there, he saw an attractive young woman, the minister's 23-year-old daughter, Ellen Axson. Ellen was an aspiring artist who

Love Letters

Woodrow wrote to Ellen in one letter, "I have found out now what it meant that I was once reserved, sensitive, morbid, and almost cold. It meant that I had never begun to live. . . . I am so glad that I am young so that I can give my youth to you."

In another letter, he said, "You are the only person in the world—except for my dear ones at home—with whom I do not have to act a part, to whom I do not have to deal out confidences cautiously."

☆☆☆

had studied at a private school in town. For the past three years, she had been caring for her father after the death of her mother.

Woodrow called at the Axson home. The Reverend Samuel Axson thought the young man had come to visit him. When Woodrow kept asking about Ellen, the pastor finally realized that the young man had come to see his daughter and invited Ellen to join them. Before he left for home, Wilson was certain that he loved Ellen. He wrote letters to her and returned to Rome several times to visit her.

Young Ellen Axson Wilson. The Wilsons were married in 1885.

In September 1883, Woodrow was changing trains in Asheville, North Carolina, when he met Ellen, who was waiting to catch a train for home. He persuaded her to delay her departure so that they could spend some time together. Later, he took her to meet members of his family, who were staying at a nearby resort. The next day, before Ellen left to go home, Woodrow asked her to marry him, and she accepted. No date was set because Woodrow was about to set off on another educational adventure. He hoped soon to be able to support a wife.

A Professor in Training ———————————

After little more than a year in Atlanta, Wilson settled on a new plan—to become a teacher at a college or university. He applied to the Johns Hopkins University in Baltimore, Maryland, to take advanced courses in politics and history. Johns Hopkins was a pioneering graduate school that emphasized scholarly research and encouraged its students to make new contributions to knowledge. Among its classes, Hopkins offered seminars, where a small group of students could discuss the topics they were studying with a professor. Wilson would bring ideas from the Johns Hopkins programs to his future academic posts.

Wilson was disappointed in the classes there, and once again set a course of independent study. He began a major research project on the U.S. government. By the end of 1884, he had produced a book-length study called *Congressional Government*, which was published the next year by a New York publisher. The book studied the division of powers between the president and Congress in the United States and was critical of the way Congress operated.

In Wilson's mind, his book on Congress and the presidency was not just a research paper. It was related to his own goals and aspirations. Early in his studies at Johns Hopkins, he had written to Ellen, "I do feel a very real regret that I have been shut out of my heart's first—primary—ambition and purpose, which was, to take an active, if possible a leading, part in public life, and strike out for myself, if I had the ability, a statesman's career."

A Married Professor

As Wilson worked on *Congressional Government*, Woodrow and Ellen spent a very difficult year. His mother was in ill health and his father was locked in a dispute with his congregation in Wilmington. Ellen had been caring for her father, who was becoming very difficult to manage. In early 1884, he was sent to a mental hospital, and a few months later, he committed suicide. After her father's death, Ellen decided to travel to New York City to study at the Art Students League.

During one of their meetings that year, Woodrow pressed Ellen to set a date for their wedding. He was hoping to land a teaching job in 1885, and they set the wedding for June. The ceremony took place in Savannah, Georgia. Ellen's grandfather and Woodrow's father conducted the ceremony.

Wilson had not yet qualified for a degree from Johns Hopkins, but he applied for a teaching position without it. He signed to teach at Bryn Mawr College, a brand-new college for women, which was opening that fall near Philadelphia. The school had recruited many of its first teachers from Johns Hopkins. It was committed to giving women a rigorous college education. When the Wilsons arrived in September 1885, however, there were just over 40 students and almost no books in the library.

Wilson still hoped to complete the requirements for the Ph.D. (Doctor of Philosophy) degree at Johns Hopkins. The degree would make it easier for him to move to other colleges or universities and to earn higher salaries. Ellen suggested that since *Congressional Government* had been published so successfully, he should submit it to Johns Hopkins to fulfill the requirement for a long research paper. Wilson sent the book to Johns Hopkins and was pleased when the university agreed to accept the book and granted him the Ph.D.

During his years at Bryn Mawr, Woodrow learned how to teach and continued to write. He also accepted invitations to give lectures at Johns Hopkins and other colleges to add to his income. Ellen was busy as well. Their daughters Margaret and Jessie were born in 1886 and 1887; a third daughter, Eleanor, would be born in 1889, after the family left Bryn Mawr. Early in 1888, Wilson's mother, who had been ill for some time, died in North Carolina.

Gradually, Woodrow grew discontented with Bryn Mawr. He had disagreements with the dean of the college, Martha Carey Thomas, who was a strong feminist. He wrote in his journal, "Lecturing to young women of the present generation on the history and principles of politics is about as appropriate and profitable as would be lecturing to stonemasons on the evolution of fashion in dress." Finally in 1888, he received an offer to teach at Wesleyan University, a men's school in Middletown, Connecticut. "I have for a long time been hungry for a class of *men*," he wrote to a friend.

As a young professor at Bryn Mawr, Wilson grew a mustache and sideburns. Not long afterward, he shaved them off.

At Wesleyan, Wilson served as chairman of the department of history and political economy. He set up the Wesleyan House of Commons, a debating society, and helped coach the football team. He also wrote *The State*, a widely praised textbook comparing different types of governments. It was translated into many languages, including Japanese. Other books would follow.

Return to Princeton ———————————————

In 1890, Wilson received an invitation to return to Princeton as a professor. He was delighted. There he taught courses in constitutional law, international law, British law, and public administration. He had used his early years to develop an effective lecture style, and students at Princeton soon voted him the most popular teacher. One student wrote that he was "the greatest classroom lecturer I have ever heard." Once again, he also coached the football team.

Woodrow put down roots in Princeton. He had a large home built for his family and the many relatives who came to visit or to stay. To help pay for it, he wrote articles for *Harper's Weekly*, a leading national magazine, and gave guest lectures. In the summer of 1893, Wilson gave an important speech on education at the World's Columbian Exposition. He argued that students should study the great books of Western civilization before they specialize in law, religion, or medicine.

Wilson gave one of his most famous speeches at the 150th anniversary of Princeton's founding, in 1896. Called "Princeton in the Nation's Service," it urged that students be educated for public service and the responsibilities of

The World's Columbian Exposition

The World's Columbian Exposition in Chicago in 1893 offered many attractions, including the world's
first Ferris wheel (in background) and lectures by many influential thinkers, including Woodrow Wilson.

The World's Columbian Exposition in Chicago celebrated the 400th anniversary of Columbus's discovery of the

New World. More than 27 million visitors came to the great "White City," a collection of elaborate temporary

buildings that housed exhibits along the shore of Chicago's Lake Michigan. Electricity ran the fair's industrial

exhibits and lit its buildings and fountains, amazing many visitors from farms and small towns where electric-

ity was not yet in use.

The fair helped popularize a host of new products, including Juicy Fruit gum, shredded wheat cereal,

soda pop, hot dogs, and hamburgers. The Midway included the first Ferris Wheel, which was 250 feet (75

meters) high, and shows where belly dancers performed the "hootchy-kootch." Marching bands and sym-

phony orchestras performed. At the same time, the fair scheduled more than 6,000 lectures on a wide variety

of subjects. Woodrow Wilson was one of the influential people invited to speak.

leadership. On this occasion, the institution officially changed its name from College of New Jersey to Princeton University.

Wilson and World Affairs

In 1898, the United States declared war on Spain to gain independence for Cuba, then a Spanish possession. U.S. military forces won a quick victory, gaining independence for Cuba and gaining new possessions for itself, including Puerto Rico, Guam, and the Philippine Islands.

For Wilson, the war was a great moment in American history. He argued that the United States had "gone out upon the seas, where nations are rivals and we cannot live or act apart." Unlike many Americans at the time, he favored greater involvement with the rest of the world.

Fast Facts
THE SPANISH-AMERICAN WAR

Who: The U.S. against Spain

When: April 1898 to August 1898

Why: U.S. opposition to Spanish rule in Cuba and public sympathy for Cuban independence; pressure to protect American investment; the destruction of the U.S. battleship *Maine*

Where: Naval battle at Manila, the Philippines; invasion of Cuba; capture of Puerto Rico

Outcome: The U.S. defeated Spanish land and sea forces in Cuba and the Philippines; the Treaty of Paris granted Cuban independence, ceded Puerto Rico and Guam to the U.S., sold the Philippines to the U.S. for $20 million

Wilson was the highest-paid Princeton professor, but he was dissatisfied. He did not think that his abilities were "stretched to their right measure." By speaking to and consulting with Princeton alumni and by developing an excellent reputation on and off campus as a professor, writer, and speaker, he laid the groundwork for another step forward in his career.

Chapter 3

President of Princeton —————————

In 1902, the president of Princeton resigned. The college's board of trustees unanimously chose star professor Woodrow Wilson to be the next president. He was the first president who was not a Presbyterian minister, and he was eager to make the college a leading institution of learning in the United States.

By this time, Wilson's aged father was living in Princeton with his son's family. He had become frail and short-tempered in his old age, but he was proud of his son's accomplishments as a scholar and teacher, and he enjoyed his son's appointment as president. A few months after Wilson took office, his father died.

Wilson soon began a series of reforms at Princeton. He had long realized that the school made only modest demands on its students. Many were there mainly to make friends and to party. Wilson

Wilson began teaching at Princeton in 1890. In 1902, he became president of the university.

raised entrance requirements for new students. He encouraged professors to make current students work harder. Later, Wilson hired young faculty members who served as preceptors, meeting with small groups of students to discuss course work. Wilson wanted to encourage students to think for themselves rather than repeating what they heard in lectures. He hoped that these discussion groups would transform the university "from a place where there are youngsters doing tasks to a place where there are men thinking, men who are conversing about the things of thought."

In May 1906, Wilson suffered bleeding in his left eye and temporarily could not see out of it. He and his family traveled to England that summer, where he rested and regained his strength. He returned to Princeton more eager than ever to accomplish his plans for reform. In 1907, Ellen proudly repeated a line from a

A Private Man

In public, Wilson usually seemed stern and solemn. With his family, he was more relaxed. His daughters and in-laws enjoyed his puns (plays on words) and his comic imitations of drunks, vain Englishmen, and villains. They welcomed the addition of his tenor voice to family sing-alongs.

His family tried not to trouble him with small concerns. Ellen did not allow him to be interrupted when he worked in his study. She managed the household accounts and chores to give him more time for research and writing. Ellen was more sociable than her husband, and when they entertained, she helped make their dinner guests feel welcome. Wilson's one regular chore was to wind the household clocks.

Wilson had simple tastes. For breakfast, he drank herbal tea and ate eggs that had been boiled for half an hour. He spent his mornings working. He used a typewriter to type out his lectures and speeches, using only a few fingers. In the afternoons he took a break to bicycle, or play tennis or billiards. Afterward, he worked again until nine o'clock, then joined in family activities.

☆ ☆ ☆

New York newspaper stating that Wilson "had ruined what was universally admitted to be the most agreeable and aristocratic country club in America by transforming it into an institution of learning."

In 1908, Wilson turned his attention to reforming social life at Princeton. He proposed to organize the campus into four quadrangles, each with its own dormitories and eating facilities. One of his aims was to replace the eating clubs, which were the most important social organizations on the campus. He felt that competition to gain membership in the clubs and their closed social activities interfered with learning. Students who did not gain membership in an eating club found it difficult to participate in other campus activities.

Wilson's plan caused a storm of protest. Graduates, who remembered their eating clubs with great affection, threatened to stop contributing money to the school. They insisted that eating clubs were an important tradition, but Wilson refused to compromise.

As this battle was continuing, Wilson got involved in another. The college was planning to construct a new and enlarged graduate school. Wilson wanted it in the middle of the campus, where it could help encourage undergraduates to pursue their studies more seriously. The dean of the graduate school, Andrew West, favored a site at the far edge of the campus, where graduate students could study without the distractions of other college activities. Wilson and West carried their fight to the college trustees and to prominent alumni. Finally, a wealthy alumnus died and left a huge sum to build the graduate school at the edge of the campus. Wilson knew he was defeated.

In danger of losing two long-term battles, Wilson began considering opportunities beyond the walls of Princeton.

Running for Governor

The popular political magazine *Harper's Weekly* had published Wilson's essays for years. The editor and publisher in 1910, George B. M. Harvey, was impressed with Wilson's energy and talent. Harvey was active in New Jersey Democratic politics, and he thought the Princeton president would make a fine candidate for governor. Harvey suggested that he could arrange for Wilson to have the Democratic nomination for governor in 1910, and Wilson agreed to give the proposal "serious consideration."

The New Jersey Democratic party was divided between old-fashioned machine politicians, who controlled the big cities, and small-town members who favored reform. Harvey had good connections with both factions. He had worked closely with party *bosses* James Smith and James Nugent, who controlled Newark, the state's largest city, and surrounding Essex County. Even though they were machine politicians, they saw Wilson as no threat to their power and agreed to back him.

Wilson won the nomination for governor on September 15, 1910. He announced to voters, "I shall enter . . . office . . . with absolutely no pledges of any kind to prevent me from serving the people." He promised to reform New Jersey politics, to improve public transportation and public services, and to protect

In 1910, Wilson ran for governor of New Jersey. This portrait of his family was used in the campaign. It includes his wife Ellen (seated next to him) and his three grown daughters, Eleanor (left), Jessie (front center), and Margaret (right).

workers against harsh working conditions. He had reformed Princeton; now he

was part of a much larger reform movement that was sweeping America.

The Progressive Movement

In the early 1900s, voters in many part of the country began clamoring for major reforms. They became known as Progressives. They wanted government to take a stronger hand in regulating business, outlawing unfair business practices and increasing competition. They also wanted government regulation of railway rates and protection for injured workmen. They urged action to assure wholesome food and safe medicines.

The movement also fought for reforms within government. In many states they enacted *direct primaries*, elections where voters chose party nominees for office; *recalls*, special votes to remove public officials from office; *referendums*, in which voters could reject an unpopular law; and *initiatives*, in which voters could enact new laws without approval of the legislature. They also favored *direct election* of U.S. senators (who were then elected by state legislatures). Many of these progressive reforms were enacted and remain in effect today.

☆ ☆ ☆

On election day, Wilson was elected governor of New Jersey for a two-year term. He received 234,000 votes to 185,000 for his Republican opponent. Democrats also gained a majority in the lower house of the New Jersey legislature. The state had no official home for its governor, so the Wilson family continued to live in Princeton. The new governor traveled 11 miles (18 kilometers) each day to Trenton, the state capital, to conduct the state's business.

Bosses Smith and Nugent expected the new governor to help them advance their own political careers. Smith wanted Wilson's support in his own run for the U.S. Senate from New Jersey. (Senators were then elected by state legislatures). However, Democrats in New Jersey had shown a clear preference for another candidate, James Martine. Wilson shocked Smith by throwing his support to Martine, who gained election. Later, Wilson replaced James Nugent as chairman of the state Democratic party. Both Smith and Nugent accused Wilson of ingratitude, and they planned to get even in the next statewide election.

Reforming New Jersey

No longer relying on the politicians who helped him win office, Wilson took personal charge of the governorship. He made appearances before the legislature to explain his views and defend his proposals. He made friendly appeals to progressive Republicans as well as Democrats. At one gathering, Wilson even danced the cakewalk with a Republican senator! Wilson also made some important new appointments. Joseph P. Tumulty, an experienced politician from Essex County, became the governor's personal secretary and took charge of filling appointive jobs in the state government. Tumulty would remain at Wilson's side for many years. His practical political advice was especially valuable, since Wilson was serving in elective office for the first time.

From January to May 1911, Wilson presented the New Jersey legislature with an ambitious program of progressive legislation. He proposed to reform election processes in the state. To protect workers, he proposed a new statewide system to pay benefits to those injured on the job. To regulate energy companies in the state, he wanted a public utilities commission to establish reasonable rates for gas and electricity. In addition, he requested a commission to regulate the rates and services of railroads.

Progressive legislators from both parties responded to Wilson's proposals. They helped pass every one of Wilson's major programs. "I got everything I strove for—and more besides," he crowed. His success gained national recognition and made Wilson a hero of the progressive movement.

As it turned out, Wilson was wise to pass his reform legislation quickly. That fall, Smith, Nugent, and other conservative Democrats refused to work for the re-election of progressive candidates. Many Democrats lost their seats, and conservative Republicans took their places. When the legislature met in January 1912, Wilson's progressive program was in trouble. Instead of passing new progressive legislation, it passed legislation to cancel the programs passed the year before. Wilson was forced to use his *veto* (refusal to sign a bill into law) to protect his progressive programs. In a few months, he refused to sign 57 bills into law.

The Presidential Candidate

Even as he fought to protect his progressive gains in New Jersey, Wilson was looking ahead.

As a leader of progressive Democrats, he began making speeches to progressive organizations across the country. "Wherever I go they seem to like me—men of all kinds and classes," he wrote with pride.

Wilson and his advisers were exploring the possibility that he might gain the Democratic nomination for president in 1912. That spring he ran strongly in Democratic primary elections. In fact, by the time the Democratic National Convention met in Baltimore in June to nominate a candidate for president, Wilson had won the support of a third of the delegates (support by two thirds was needed for the nomination).

The Democratic party was badly split, however, and many of its strongest supporters were not progressives. When the voting for the presidential nomination began, Wilson ran a poor second to "Champ" Clark, a former Speaker of the House of Representatives, but no candidate had nearly enough votes to win.

Finally, on the 14th ballot, the leader of the party's liberal wing, William Jennings Bryan, helped settle the issue. Bryan, a champion of many reformist causes, had been the Democratic candidate for president three times (1896, 1900, and 1908) and had lost each time. Now he threw his support to Wilson as the most promising reformer in the race. With this new support, Wilson finally gained the required two-thirds majority on the 46th ballot. He later learned that his managers gained Indiana's votes by promising the vice-presidential nomination to Indiana governor Thomas Marshall.

Meanwhile, the Republicans were even more divided than the Democrats. Former president Theodore Roosevelt was fighting hard for the nomination against his former friend, President William Howard Taft. When the national convention nominated Taft, Roosevelt and his supporters walked out and formed the Progressive party. It nominated Roosevelt for president.

With Republicans split between two strong candidates, the Democrats had a golden opportunity to elect the first Democratic president in 20 years. The real contest was between the two progressives, Roosevelt and Wilson. Roosevelt ran a vigorous campaign. Yet without the support of his Republican party, he did not have local organizations to campaign locally and help get out the vote. Wilson was more progressive in his views than many in his party, but the Democrats were united behind him, hoping to elect a Democratic president.

On election day, Wilson received 6.3 million popular votes to Roosevelt's 4.1 million and Taft's 3.5 million. In the electoral college, Wilson's victory was overwhelming. He received 435 electoral votes to Roosevelt's 88 and Taft's 8. Democrats also won a majority of seats in Congress. Wilson did not have a strong

In the presidential election of 1912, former president Theodore Roosevelt (far left) ran on the Progressive party ticket. President William Howard Taft (left) was the Republican nominee. When Roosevelt and Taft split the Republican vote, Woodrow Wilson (above) became the first Democrat to be elected president in 20 years.

mandate from the voters—he had won less than half of the popular vote. Still, he was confident that he would succeed in the office he believed he was always meant to hold.

Wilson's Domestic Program

On March 4, 1913, Woodrow Wilson was sworn in as the 28th U.S. president. He told Americans, "This is not a day of triumph; it is a day of dedication." As at Princeton and in the New Jersey State House, he was ready to propose important reforms and to help get them passed. He summoned Congress to meet in a special session on April 7. The next day, to the lawmakers' surprise, he appeared personally to outline his plan for reform. No president since Thomas Jefferson had appeared personally for a legislative session. Wilson outlined a program that would keep Congress at work for 18 straight months, its longest single session up to that time.

First on Wilson's agenda was the reduction of *tariffs*, taxes on products made abroad and brought to the United States for sale. He believed that reduced tariffs would encourage world trade and help

Wilson gives his inaugural address in March 1913. Outgoing president Taft is seated at the right.

the economy. In addition, they would be popular in the solidly Democratic South, which had always favored low tariffs. Congress passed the Underwood-Simmons Tariff Act, which reduced tariff rates.

In June, Wilson asked Congress to approve a major reform of the money and banking system. Six months later, Congress passed legislation establishing the Federal Reserve System, an organization that includes twelve regional banks governed by a board of bankers and businessmen appointed by the president. The system, which remains in place today, serves as a banking agent for the federal government and regulates the currency. By controlling interest rates, the Federal Reserve also helps regulate private banks. Wilson also approved the first income Tax, which was made possible by the ratification of the Sixteenth Amendment in 1913. (An earlier income tax law had been ruled unconstitutional by the U.S. Supreme Court.)

In the area of regulating business, Wilson asked Congress for a new antitrust law that would clarify and enlarge the Sherman Antitrust Act of 1890. In 1914, Congress passed the Clayton Act, which outlawed certain actions by a business aimed at establishing a *monopoly* (complete control of its industry). The act also broadened the rights of labor unions. In a companion law, Congress established the Federal Trade Commission, a regulatory body designed to discourage development of business monopolies and to investigate unfair trade practices.

A Strong President ——————————————————

Once again, Wilson was demonstrating his ability to get things done and to help make significant reforms. The office of the president still had only a small staff and a smaller budget. As a result, Wilson did much of the work himself. He had no speechwriters, so he wrote his own speeches, usually in shorthand. Often, he typed them out on his own typewriter. Fortunately, Wilson had some very able advisers and assistants. Joe Tumulty came with Wilson from New Jersey to serve as his chief aide, combining such modern jobs as press secretary, appointments secretary, and chief of staff.

For private advice, Wilson turned increasingly to Colonel Edward M. House. Wilson described House as a "truly disinterested friend" who wanted nothing for himself. He wrote to House, "You are the only person in the world with whom I can discuss everything." House refused to accept an appointment to direct a department of the government, which would make him a member of the *cabinet*, the group that officially advises the president. Instead, he advised Wilson unofficially, offering suggestions on appointments and negotiating with leaders in Congress.

Wilson poses with his friend and adviser Colonel Edward House.

Wilson appointed Albert S. Burleson postmaster general, the cabinet member then responsible for appointing hundreds of party members to important government jobs. William Jennings Bryan became secretary of state, and Wilson's future son-in-law William Gibbs McAdoo was named secretary of the treasury. Wilson also asked for advice from others outside Washington. Louis Brandeis, a progressive lawyer in Boston, offered suggestions on legislation to

Colonel Edward House

Edward House (1858–1938) was a wealthy Texan who had played an influential role in the careers of several Texas politicians. In 1910, he moved to New York, hoping to be helpful to the national Democratic party. The next year, he met Woodrow Wilson, and the two soon became friends. House concluded that this progressive governor of New Jersey could become a new Democratic leader and might be elected president.

At the 1912 Democratic convention, House worked behind the scenes to bring about Wilson's nomination for president. He helped persuade William Jennings Bryan to shift his support to Wilson during the voting and may have helped make deals with other leading politicians to ensure Wilson's success.

House would continue to advise Wilson through most of his presidency. Increasingly he concentrated on foreign affairs, making several trips to Europe before and during the Great War as Wilson's personal representative.

☆ ☆ ☆

control monopolies and to protect workers against exploitation. Wilson later appointed Brandeis to the U.S. Supreme Court, making him the first Jewish justice in court history.

The president also consulted regularly with congressional leaders and had a private telephone line installed to communicate with them. He sent Postmaster General Burleson and others to Congress to help negotiate passage of legislation.

Wilson encouraged cabinet members to take responsibility for their own departments. This caused some unfortunate results. Secretaries Burleson and McAdoo established rules segregating African Americans from other workers and treating them unfairly. Wilson himself believed this policy was "in the interest of the colored people, as exempting them from friction and criticism." A recently formed civil rights group, the National Association for the Advancement of Colored People (NAACP), protested the discrimination, and Wilson required Burleson and McAdoo to change their policies.

Family Joys and Sorrows

Woodrow and Ellen Wilson saw two of their three daughters married in the White House. In 1913 their second daughter, Jessie, married a teacher, Francis B. Sayre. When they left to settle in Massachusetts, Wilson said, "I feel bereaved." Six months later, the Wilsons' third daughter, Eleanor, was married to

Ellen Wilson helped plan the wedding of two of her daughters in the White House. Then in 1914, she fell ill and died on August 6 of kidney disease.

Secretary of the Treasury McAdoo. Daughter Margaret chose to pursue a singing career.

In 1914, soon after the second wedding, Ellen Wilson sickened. She was diagnosed with Bright's disease, a serious kidney disorder. After a painful illness, she died on August 6, 1914. The brokenhearted Wilson told Colonel House that he was no longer fit to be president. He said that he "did not think straight any longer and had no heart for the things he was doing." However, events refused to wait on a grieving president. Wilson had foreign policy problems to solve.

Mexico

In foreign affairs, Wilson faced a difficult and confusing situation in Mexico. Before Wilson's inauguration, General Victoriano Huerta took control of Mexico. He threw out the elected government and established a dictatorship. Wilson refused to recognize Huerta's government and quietly encouraged Huerta's opponent, the reformer Venustiano Carranza.

In April 1914, Huerta's army officers arrested and imprisoned some American sailors who were ashore in Tampico, a port city on the Gulf of Mexico. Wilson used this "insult" to U.S. sailors as an excuse to send U.S. troops to occupy Veracruz, Mexico's most important port on the Gulf of Mexico. Huerta

Pancho Villa

Pancho Villa (1878–1923) grew up in the Mexican state of Durango. He became an outlaw, and a folk hero because (like Robin Hood) he stole from rich landowners and gave to the poor. Villa was once an ally of Venustiano Carranza, but later changed his mind and used his army against Carranza's government. Villa kept his ragtag troops together by stealing cattle in Mexico and selling them in the United States.

Pancho Villa, a leader of the ongoing Mexican Revolution, invaded a town in New Mexico in 1916, causing the Wilson administration to send troops into northern Mexico to find Villa. Villa was never caught, but he did not raid U.S. territory again.

★★☆

was forced to resign in July, and Carranza took power. In the next few years, he managed to enact a new constitution for Mexico.

Carranza's rule continued to be threatened, however. Radicals demanding more reforms mobilized rebel armies to overthrow his government. Pancho Villa was the leader of a radical army in northern Mexico. In 1916, his forces raided the small settlement of Columbus, New Mexico, killing 17 U.S. citizens. Villa hoped that the United States would declare war on Mexico, causing the downfall of the Carranza government. Instead, Wilson dispatched an army under General John J. Pershing to enter northern Mexico to capture Villa and bring him to justice. After a seven-month search and many casualties, the U.S. forces withdrew without finding Villa.

Early moviemakers in Hollywood made a hero of Pancho Villa, releasing a film biography of him in 1914. After his raid on Columbus, New Mexico, in 1916, Villa went underground and avoided capture by U.S. troops in Mexico. In 1920, he signed a peace agreement with a new Mexican government. In 1923 he was assassinated.

European Diplomacy

On August 4, 1914, two days before Ellen Wilson died, war broke out in Europe. This so-called Great War was later known as World War I. On one side were the Central Powers, which included Germany and Austria-Hungary. On the other side were the Allied Powers, which included France, Great Britain, and Russia. For nearly four and a half years, these main combatants would carry on a war more widespread and more deadly than any other in earlier history.

Allied soldiers occupy a trench in a damaged and deserted village in present-day Belgium during World War I.

The United States had a long tradition of isolation from European conflicts. Even before the war, Wilson had sent Colonel House to Europe in an effort to ease tensions between countries. Now he sent House back to see if some settlement or cease-fire might be possible. At home, Wilson counseled Americans to be "impartial in thought as well as in action." He even drafted a message to be shown in movie theaters, asking the audience not to applaud or boo scenes from the war.

U.S. Neutrality and German Submarine Policy

Britain tried to blockade Germany, cutting off the delivery of food and munitions by sea. It seized merchant ships of any nation, including the United States, but according to the rules of war, it paid for the cargoes it took and released the seamen. The Germans retaliated by declaring the waters around Britain to be a war zone. It sent submarines to attack Allied merchant shipping. German submarine commanders began torpedoing ships without allowing their crews to escape, as traditional naval warfare demanded. Then in May 1915, a German submarine torpedoed and sank the *Lusitania*, a British luxury liner, off the coast of Ireland.

President Wilson sent angry notes to the Germans protesting the sinking of a passenger ship. To avoid the danger that the United States might enter the war, Germany agreed to change its submarine tactics against neutral and passenger ships. Republicans in Congress urged Wilson to begin to prepare the nation for war, but he resisted their pressure. In a famous response, he urged America to become an example of peace. "There is such a thing as a nation being too proud to fight," he said.

Sinking the *Lusitania*

The luxury liner *Lusitania* was sunk by German submarines in May 1915. The incident brought the United States closer to war with Germany.

The British luxury passenger ship *Lusitania* left New York for Liverpool, England, on May 1, 1915, carrying nearly 2,000 people. Owners of the ship believed that if German submarines attacked, the *Lusitania*'s speed would protect her. Off the Irish coast, however, a fog settled in, and *Lusitania* reduced its speed for safety. The ship's captain, who had been advised to take a zigzag course, sailed straight through the fog. A German submarine found the *Lusitania* on May 7, near Kinsale, Ireland. It scored a direct torpedo hit. Soon afterward there was a second explosion deep in the *Lusitania*, perhaps caused by ammunition being secretly shipped to Britain. The giant liner sank in only 18 minutes. In the confusion, there was time to launch only 6 of the ship's 48 lifeboats. Nearly 1,200 men, women, and children, including 128 Americans, lost their lives.

Fast Facts

WORLD WAR I

Who: The Central Powers (including Germany and Austria-Hungary) against the Allied Powers (including Britain, France, Russia, and later the U.S.)

When: August 1914 to November 1918

Why: Long-simmering rivalries between nations were ignited by the assassination of an heir to the Austro-Hungarian throne in July 1914; the U.S. declared war in April 1917 after Germany announced unrestricted submarine warfare in Allied waters.

Where: Major battles in Belgium and northern France; along the German-Russian border; along the Austrian-Italian border; and in the Middle East

Outcome: The retreating German army requested an armistice (cease-fire) in November 1918. The war was officially ended by the Treaty of Versailles, signed in June 1919. The treaty reduced the size of Germany and broke up Austria-Hungary, establishing several new countries. It also established the League of Nations, a world organization to settle international disputes.

The next year, the unarmed steamer *Sussex*, which carried passengers across the English Channel between Britain and France, was sunk without warning by a German torpedo. Wilson, infuriated that Germany had broken its promises, threatened to break off diplomatic relations. Once again, the Germans promised to follow the rules of war and to end surprise attacks.

Remarriage and Re-election

Dealing with the increasingly serious war in Europe was difficult for Wilson, who was lonely and still mourning the death of his wife. In March 1915, Dr. Cary Grayson, the White

House physician, came to the rescue. He arranged for Wilson to meet an attractive Washington widow, Edith Bolling Galt. The president soon began to invite Mrs. Galt to dinner and took long drives with her. A Secret Service man realized that Wilson was in love when he heard the president whistling the latest hit tune, "Oh! You Beautiful Doll."

Wilson proposed to Edith Galt in May 1915, and in September, she agreed to their engagement. "How empty the hours are without you!" he wrote to her during these months. He began sending her government memos, and she started to offer him advice on government policy, even though she had only three years of formal education.

Wilson's advisers, including McAdoo and Tumulty, advised the president to put off his wedding. In a day when widowed partners were expected to mourn for several years, they feared that his remarriage would cost him votes in the 1916 presidential election. Wilson considered the advice but refused to accept it. The couple announced their engagement in October and were married quietly in Edith's home on December 18, 1915.

That same month, the president asked Congress for money to build more ships for the navy, to increase the regular army, and to create an independent reserve force of 40,000 men to replace the National Guard. To win support for his

President Wilson took time out in April 1916 to throw out the first ball, opening the major league baseball season. His new wife Edith (in the hat with a bow) enjoys the moment.

preparedness program, Wilson presented his views on a speaking tour in February 1916. Congress agreed to strengthen the navy and the army but refused the request for an independent reserve force.

During the 1916 presidential election campaign, Wilson focused on his progressive policies. His supporters also defended his wartime policies. They used the slogan "He Kept Us Out of War," hoping to attract voters who were against entering the European conflict. The Republicans, united again, nominated Supreme Court Justice Charles Evans Hughes, who resigned from the court to run for president. It was a close contest, and on election night, Wilson spoke to his assistant on the phone before he went to bed. "Well, Tumulty," he said, "it begins to look as if we were badly licked."

Four days later, when final results were reported from the western states, Wilson learned that he had been re-elected. He received about 600,000 more popular votes than Hughes, but the result in the electoral college was very close. Wilson gained 277 votes to Hughes's 254. Wilson had won a second term, which would prove to be a severe trial to him and to the nation.

Chapter 5

America Goes to War

On April 6, 1917, only five months after his re-election, President Wilson asked Congress to declare war on the Central Powers. In his address, he said, "The world must be made safe for democracy." By that time, a majority of citizens supported American entry into the war. In a few months, many things had changed.

In January, the Germans had resumed unrestricted submarine warfare. They hoped to cut off all shipments of food and war supplies to Great Britain, and they believed that the British would be forced to surrender within five months. The new policy also threatened U.S. ships that were delivering supplies to the British. President Wilson broke off diplomatic relations with Germany, bringing war closer.

Late in February, the president learned of an amazing telegram that the British had intercepted. It was sent by German foreign secretary Arthur Zimmermann to Germany's ambassador in Mexico. The message informed the ambassador that unlimited submarine warfare might bring the United States into the war. It instructed the ambassador to form an alliance with Mexico against the United States. If the United States declared war, the Mexicans would agree to attack along the U.S.–Mexican border. In return for its support, Mexico would receive the U.S. states of Texas, New Mexico, and Arizona when Germany and her allies won the war. The Zimmermann Telegram was made public on March 1, causing a firestorm of anger against the Germans.

Later in March, bad news from Russia caused increased concern about a possible German victory. Revolutionaries in Petrograd (present-day St. Petersburg) forced the Russian czar to abdicate (give up his rights and powers). Within days, hundreds of thousands of Russian troops stopped fighting the invading German army. This allowed the Germans to shift more troops to France, where they hoped to defeat the French and British and win the war.

The danger of a victory by Germany and its allies persuaded President Wilson that the United States must enter the war and provide much needed support to Britain and France. At his request, Congress passed the declaration of war on April 6, 1917. In May, Wilson signed an act creating a draft system under which 2.5 million men would soon be called for military service.

On April 2, 1917, only a month after gaining reelection, Wilson addresses a joint session of Congress to request a declaration of war against Germany. Congress passed the declaration days later.

Preparations to fight were slow. Troops had to be called up and trained. Ships, vehicles, weapons, and ammunition had to be manufactured. U.S. commanders hoped to have troops in battle by May 1918. Meanwhile, the war in Europe continued to claim thousands of lives each week. In November, Russia withdrew from the war altogether after Communist hard-liners gained control of the government.

The Home Front at War

At home, the government mounted a campaign urging civilians to support the war effort. Most Americans agreed to limit their diets, eating no meat on one day each week and no bread on another to conserve food, which would be shipped to Europe. The Wilsons made a special symbolic contribution to the campaign. Sheep grazed on the White House lawn, and their wool was auctioned off to aid the war effort.

Wilson was active in many war-related activities. He created the Inquiry, a group of experts to advise him on all issues relating to the war. He also helped establish special organizations to manage wartime production, prevent work stoppages, increase farm output, and accomplish many other important tasks.

Wilson also supported harsh new laws against possible traitors in the United States. The Espionage Act of 1917 imposed stiff fines and long jail terms

The mobilization for war had one unexpected result at home. Early in 1917, Wilson received a visit from Carrie Chapman Catt, the president of the largest women's suffrage organization. Her group had voted to support the president if he declared war on Germany. At the same time, it was hoping that Wilson would support a constitutional amendment to give women the vote.

Grateful for the suffrage movement's support of the war, and pressured to take a stand by his wife and daughters, Wilson agreed to help. In January 1918, he publicly urged Congress to pass the women's suffrage amendment as an important part of the war effort. The Nineteenth Amendment received final approval by Congress in May 1919 and was approved by the required three-quarters of the states in August 1920.

A supporter of voting rights for women pickets the White House early in 1917. Soon afterward, Wilson announced his support for woman suffrage.

☆☆☆

for anyone convicted of spying, sabotage, or refusing military service. The Alien Act of 1918 allowed noncitizens to be deported without trial if they were suspected of disloyalty. The Sedition Act, also passed in 1918, permitted citizens to be jailed if they spoke out against the government or the armed forces.

The passions stirred up by the war led to persecution of German Americans and others suspected of disloyalty. Crowds attacked Americans of German descent (and others with German-sounding names). Many Americans refused to eat German foods, listen to German music, or even buy dogs with German names (such as dachshunds). Others who were attacked included *pacifists* (those who opposed all wars) and members of socialist and other "radical" political parties.

War Aims

Even before U.S. troops went into combat in Europe, President Wilson called a joint session of Congress on January 8, 1918. In his most famous address, the president presented the nation's war aims, "Fourteen Points" that he believed could lead to lasting peace in the world.

The first four points outlined broad policies that would revolutionize the way governments dealt with each other. The first point called for "open covenants of peace, openly arrived at," rather than secret agreements between major powers.

The second called for "absolute freedom of navigation upon the seas." The third called for "the removal . . . of all economic barriers and the establishment of an equality of trade conditions." The fourth called for "adequate guarantees . . . that national armaments will be reduced."

Points five through thirteen outlined Wilson's plan for establishing new national borders after the war. He insisted that peoples in disputed territories were entitled to *self-determination,* the right to help determine the boundaries and leadership of their countries. One by one, he outlined policies concerning Russia, Belgium, territories disputed by France and Germany, Italy, Austria-Hungary, the Balkan states, Turkey, and Poland.

The fourteenth and final point became the most famous and controversial. Wilson said, "A general association of nations must be formed . . . for the purpose of affording mutual guarantees of political independence and territorial integrity to great and small states alike." Wilson believed that an international "League of Nations" could help settle disputes between countries and reduce the danger of future wars.

Wilson's ambitious outline for peace was welcomed by common citizens and political thinkers alike. Millions came to believe that the Fourteen Points could bring a new start in world affairs and could prevent another terrible war. The plan made Wilson an international hero.

The Cost of War

Before peace could be negotiated, however, the war had to be won. In May 1918, U.S. armies went into combat against Germany alongside veteran British and French armies. An increasing stream of war supplies from the United States was already helping Allied forces. Now the "Yanks," as they were called, proved themselves in battle. During the summer, they helped halt German advances at Château-Thierry and Belleau Wood. They led a successful counteroffensive in the Argonne Forest from late September to early November. Finally, on November 11, 1918, the German government asked for an armistice to end the fighting.

The war had been a brutal bloodbath for both sides. Germany, Austria-Hungary, and their allies suffered more than 3 million dead and 8.5 million wounded or missing. Britain, France, Russia, and their allies suffered nearly 5 million dead and nearly 13 million wounded. Of these, about 50,000 dead and 200,000 wounded were Americans. No one can calculate how many millions of civilians died in four and a half years of fighting.

Peacemaking

The peace conference to bring an official end to the war was scheduled to meet near Paris, France, in December 1918. President Wilson decided to break with tradition and attend the conference in person. On December 4, 1918, he sailed to

U.S. troops in action in France during 1918.

Europe with his wife and his advisers. He was the first president to travel across the Atlantic while holding office.

The American delegation to the peace conference was made up of close advisers to the president, including his close friend, Colonel House. It did not include any Republican leaders, even though Republicans had gained majorities in Congress in the 1918 elections. The president was determined to negotiate with world leaders personally, without interference from other Americans.

Wilson was greeted in Europe by cheering crowds, who hoped that he could help restore peace and bring a safer world. The leaders of the European powers were not so hopeful. They respected Wilson's ideals, but they were interested in practical matters, such as protecting their territories from future invasions and gaining payments from the defeated nations to help rebuild their countries.

On February 14, 1919, Wilson presented a draft charter for his League of Nations to the peace conference. He described the new international organization as "a definite guarantee against the things which have just come near bringing the whole structure of civilization into ruin." The other leaders at the conference received the proposal with respect, but not with enthusiasm. The French premier, Georges Clemenceau, considered Wilson a dreamer. When he read the Fourteen Points, he remarked privately, "God himself was content with ten commandments. Wilson modestly inflicted fourteen on us."

President Wilson waves to cheering crowds in Paris in December 1918. He was there to participate in the Versailles peace conference.

Later in February, Wilson sailed back to the United States to deal with political matters at home. He left Colonel House in charge of the U.S. delegation. When he returned to Europe in March, Wilson found that House had made many concessions on the peace treaty. He had agreed to European demands to divide German and Austro-Hungarian territories and to force the defeated nations to pay *reparations*, large payments over many years for war damages. Wilson was upset by House's actions, and their close friendship was never quite the same. Wilson accepted the concessions House had agreed to, but he became more determined than ever to hold out for the League of Nations.

In April, the president became seriously ill. Dr. Grayson reported that he had the flu, but he may have had a small stroke (bleeding in the brain). After he recovered, the president seemed far less willing to make further concessions on the peace agreement. By June, the treaty was completed. It kept the provision establishing the League of Nations, but on many other matters, it ignored Wilson's Fourteen Points. On June 28, 1919, Wilson and other world leaders signed the treaty at Versailles, the former home of French kings near Paris.

"Well, little girl," he said to Edith, "it is finished, and as no one is satisfied, it makes me hope we have made a just peace; but it is all in the lap of the gods."

The nations of the world signed the peace treaty in June 1919 at Versailles, the former residence of French kings near Paris.

The Fight for the League ———————————

On July 31, 1919, Senator Henry Cabot Lodge of Massachusetts began six weeks of Senate hearings to debate the Treaty of Versailles. According to the U.S. Constitution, the Senate was required to *ratify* (approve) a treaty by a two-thirds majority. Many Republican senators were completely opposed to American

The League of Nations

The League of Nations began operation in 1920, with its headquarters in Geneva, Switzerland. It was made up of an assembly of all the members; an executive council of five great powers and four nonpermanent members (later increased to eleven); and a secretariat to handle administration.

The league established several related groups. One was the International Labor Organization (ILO), whose aim was to improve conditions for workers around the world. Other league organizations fought disease, improved international transportation and communication, and tried to ban slavery. The league also established the World Court, which met in the Netherlands to hear disputes arising under treaties or international law.

Many powerful countries paid little attention to the League of Nations, and some (including the United States) never joined. When wars threatened, the league proved to be helpless to prevent them. In 1945, after World War II, a new world body, the United Nations, was established. It took over many of the functions of the old League of Nations.

☆ ☆ ☆

membership in the League of Nations. Lodge was a leader of Republicans who were willing to accept membership in the league, but only with *reservations* (or official restrictions). They wanted to add their own restrictions to the treaty to protect American sovereignty (the government's right to act independently), Congress's right to declare war, and other matters.

"Those senators don't know what the people are thinking," Wilson said. After negotiating unsuccessfully with the Senate for two months, he decided to appeal directly to the public. He set out on a demanding speaking tour to defend the league. In the next few weeks, he covered 8,200 miles (13,200 km) and gave 40 speeches urging Senate ratification of the treaty and U.S. membership in the League of Nations.

Republican senator Henry Cabot Lodge led the opposition to the Versailles Treaty, insisting on special reservations to protect U.S. sovereignty.

Wilson made a speaking tour to gain support for the peace settlement. In the end the Senate refused to ratify the treaty.

During the trip, Wilson suffered agonizing headaches. Finally, on September 25, after speaking in Pueblo, Colorado, he collapsed. He was not strong enough to continue the tour. His physician, Dr. Grayson, issued a press release saying that the president had suffered a breakdown and directed that the president's train speed back to Washington. Then on October 2, Wilson suffered a massive stroke, which paralyzed his left side.

Disabled President

Only Wilson's closest advisers and family knew how ill he was. Edith Wilson, Dr. Grayson, and Wilson's secretary, Joe Tumulty, took part in a cover-up, concealing his true condition. At first, they even refused to tell Vice President Thomas R. Marshall.

Years later, Edith wrote that she was most deeply concerned about her husband's health. She said one doctor warned that if Wilson was forced to resign, he would lose his will to live. Others warned that he should be shielded from any bad news. In the following weeks, Edith became the guard at the door of the president's sickroom. She decided who could visit him and what matters could be brought up with him. "I, myself, never made a single decision regarding the disposition of public affairs," she wrote. "The only decision that was mine was what was important and what was not, and the *very* important decision of when to present matters to my husband."

For a month after the president's stroke, the business of government simply stopped. Secretary of State Robert Lansing conducted cabinet meetings, but

Presidential Disability

When Wilson suffered his severe illness, the Constitution offered little guidance on how to handle a presidential disability. Secretary of State Lansing suggested that the president's aides declare him disabled and that Vice President Thomas R. Marshall serve as acting president until Wilson recovered. However, Dr. Grayson and Joe Tumulty refused to cooperate. When Marshall learned of the dispute, he made it clear he did not want to become acting president in any case. Today, the Twenty-fifth Amendment to the Constitution, approved in 1967, provides a procedure to follow when a president is disabled.

☆ ★ ☆

no important decisions were made. At the end of October, with much publicity, the King and Queen of Belgium briefly visited Wilson in his sickroom. In the meantime, Wilson's cabinet and staff prepared routine messages and proclamations that went out in the president's name.

In November 1919, Edith Wilson showed her husband the reservations Senator Lodge insisted on adding to the peace treaty. Wilson refused to accept them, and the treaty was voted down by the Senate on November 19. On December 6, two senators demanded to see Wilson. Edith hid from them how ill he was. She adjusted the lighting and covered her husband's paralyzed arm with a blanket.

By February 1920, Wilson began to take more interest in governing. One of his first acts was to dismiss Secretary of State Lansing for conducting cabinet meetings in his absence. The president still would not compromise on the treaty. He insisted that the Senate approve it as written. The treaty went down to its final defeat on March 19, 1920. Wilson told Dr. Grayson, "If I were not a Christian, I think I should go mad, but my faith in God holds me to the belief that He is in some way working out His own plans through human perversities and mistakes."

Woodrow and Edith Wilson on a brief outing during Wilson's recuperation from his serious stroke.

Frustrated Ambitions

Although his health remained delicate, Wilson dreamed of running for a third term as president. The Democratic party understood that he was not a realistic candidate, however. Wilson's health was not the only issue. The country had grown tired of Wilson's crusade for the League of Nations and was retreating from the progressive policies that helped elect him. In the summer of 1920, the

In November 1920, Republican Warren Harding was elected president. He opposed U.S. membership in the League of Nations.

Democrats nominated Ohio governor James M. Cox to run for president. The Republican nominee, Senator Warren G. Harding, won in a landslide, running on the slogan "return to normalcy."

In December, Wilson was awarded the Nobel Peace Prize in recognition of his long battle for the League of Nations. The prize recognized Wilson's great aspirations, but it also highlighted his failure. His own nation would never become a member of the world organization he helped to create.

In March 1921, a frail Woodrow Wilson rode with Warren Harding to the Capitol, where Harding would be sworn in as president. During the ceremony, Wilson left by a side door to go to his new home in Washington.

Chapter 6

Remembering Woodrow Wilson

The Final Years

Edith and Woodrow Wilson agreed that they should live in Washington after they left the White House. They bought an elegant home on S Street, where they settled in March 1921. It had been more than a year since Wilson's stroke. He had improved greatly, but he still was not well. He was bored and restless. His friends helped Wilson set up a law practice with former cabinet member Bainbridge Colby. However, Wilson refused to accept cases that used the partners' special influence as former government officials. As a result, the law firm lacked clients, and it closed its doors in 1922. In 1923, Wilson turned to writing, but he found it difficult to concentrate. Sometimes his memory failed him. When a publisher returned an article asking for revisions, he got angry and refused to make any changes.

To fill his days, Woodrow Wilson went for afternoon auto rides with his wife or other members of the family. As a distraction, Wilson looked forward to seeing movies. In the White House, these had been projected onto a sheet in the Lincoln Bedroom. In his new home, a window shade served as a screen. There the former president watched new releases and home movies of his granddaughters.

Silent Movies

One of the first films made in America was called "Fred Ott's Sneeze." First shown in 1889, it showed a man sneezing. Later films lasted several minutes, and told simple stories. In 1903, Edwin S. Porter's nine-minute *Great Train Robbery* helped popularize movies. It showed an exciting chase scene and had been filmed outdoors, rather than in a studio. By 1910, audiences enjoyed three-reel comedies, dramas, westerns, and love stories. They were still less than half an hour long and were silent, but moviemakers had learned to tell an effective story, helped along by written "titles," explaining the action or spelling out what a character was saying.

In 1915, one of the most elaborate films ever made caused a huge sensation. *The Birth of a Nation*, directed by D. W. Griffith, ran for three and a half hours. The story was set in the Civil War era and showed spectacular crowd and battle scenes. Its negative treatment of African Americans caused widespread discussion. President Wilson saw the film in the White House. He is said to have commented, "It's like history with lightning. And my only regret is that it is all terribly true."

By the early 1920s, theaters planned especially for showing films were being built in towns and cities across the country. At the same time, Woodrow Wilson became a devoted movie fan in the privacy of his own home.

The Death of a President

On November 10, 1923, the night before the fifth anniversary of the armistice that ended the Great War, Woodrow Wilson gave an address on the radio. The next day he was able to address a crowd of well-wishers outside his home, holding out hope for a better world. As the 1924 elections approached, Wilson dreamed of running once again for president. He even drafted a document summarizing the principles of the Democratic party. The party did not take his dreams seriously. As he approached his 67th birthday, he remained frail and isolated.

At 11:15 on the morning of February 3, 1924, Woodrow Wilson died at his home on S Street. A private service was held at the Wilson residence and followed by a public memorial at Washington's National Cathedral. Wilson's remains were placed in a vault inside the church.

Wilson's Place in U.S. History

Although he was elected president with less than a majority of the popular vote in 1912, Woodrow Wilson soon proved to be an active and effective president. During his first term, he helped pass more progressive legislation than any other president except Theodore Roosevelt. After Roosevelt's Republican party was taken over by more conservative members, Wilson attracted many progressive voters to the Democratic party.

Wilson died in February 1924 and was laid to rest in this tomb in the National Cathedral in Washington, D.C.

Wilson's administration helped set the federal government on a modern financial footing by establishing the Federal Reserve System and by implementing the first income tax. It strengthened regulation of big business and established the rights of labor unions through the passage of the Clayton Antitrust Act. In addition, the president supported a constitutional amendment granting women the right to vote. He was a late convert to the cause of women's suffrage, but his support helped assure the passage and ratification of the amendment.

Wilson's second term was dominated by the issues of war and peace. He tried valiantly to keep the United States out of the Great War in Europe. When circumstances changed, however, he urged a declaration of war and became an effective war president, helping to mobilize the country and to use its vast resources to help the Allied Powers win the war.

His most important contribution was his quest for international peace and order at the end of the war. Alone among the leaders of the great powers, he outlined a plan for a settlement of the war. His plan centered on the establishment of an international organization, the League of Nations, with authority to settle disputes between countries and maintain peace. For his long battle to establish the league, he earned the Nobel Peace Prize. At home, he urged the United States to take a more active role in international affairs, believing the country could no longer live in isolation from the rest of the world.

Wilson's plan for peace was not adopted. Leaders whose countries had suffered huge losses during the Great War took charge of the peace process and forced harsh treatment of the defeated nations. They did agree, however, to make Wilson's League of Nations a part of the final treaty.

The final tragedy for Wilson was that his own country would not agree to become a member of the League of Nations. He refused to compromise with leaders in the Senate, and the Senate refused to agree to membership. Not until the United Nations was formed, more than 20 years after Wilson's death, did the United States take its place in a gathering of world nations.

Wilson's failures were caused partly by flaws in his own character. He was often opinionated and prejudiced. He believed that African Americans were inferior, and he favored segregating (separating) them from whites. This view was more common in his time than it is today, but Wilson was less flexible on racial matters than many of his supporters. He also seemed reluctant to treat women as intellectual equals, and was angered by feminist leaders demanding better treatment of women. On this issue, he made some change over his lifetime, publicly supporting the right of women to vote.

Wilson was a brilliant thinker and a persuasive speaker, but in private dealings he could be stern and arrogant. He was so convinced of his own beliefs that he had difficulty seeing things from another point of view. He had trouble

President Woodrow Wilson.

compromising or acknowledging the contributions of others. It may be that some of these failings (especially late in his life) were accentuated by the illness that disabled him and later contributed to his death.

Even Wilson himself would not have considered his presidency a complete success since he failed to achieve his most cherished goals. Yet he was different from many earlier presidents. He had a powerful vision of the world as he believed it could be. His idealism and his real desire to make the world a better place made him an international hero. Even today, students of government study his writings and his speeches, inspired by his hope for a more just and a more peaceful world.

Woodrow Wilson

Birth:	December 28, 1856
Birthplace:	Staunton, Virginia
Parents:	Joseph Ruggles Wilson and Jessie Janet Woodrow Wilson
Sisters & Brothers:	Marion (1850–1890)
	Annie Josephine (1854–1916)
	Joseph Ruggles (1866–1927)
Education:	Davidson College, Davidson, North Carolina, 1873–1874
	College of New Jersey at Princeton, B.A., 1879
	University of Virginia Law School, 1879–1880
	Johns Hopkins University, 1883–1885, received Ph.D. in political science, 1886
Occupations:	College professor, university president
Marriage:	To Ellen Louise Axson, June 24, 1885
	To Edith Bolling Galt, December 18, 1915
Children:	(see First Lady Fast Facts at right)
Political Party:	Democratic
Public Offices:	1911–1913 Governor of New Jersey
	1913–1921 Twenty-eighth President of the United States
His Vice President:	Thomas Riley Marshall
Major Actions as President:	October 1913 Signed income tax and tariff reduction bills
	December 1913 Signed the Federal Reserve Act
	April 1914 Ordered the occupation of Veracruz, Mexico
	October 1914 Signed the Clayton Antitrust Act
	March 1916 Sent troops to Mexico to pursue Pancho Villa
	August 1916 Acquired the U.S. Virgin Islands from Denmark
	April 1917 Signed declaration of war against Germany
	May 1917 Signed an act creating the military draft
	January 1918 Presented the Fourteen Points to Congress
	December 1918 Participated in Versailles peace conference
	September 1919 Urged League of Nations membership
Firsts:	First president since Thomas Jefferson to address Congress in person
	First president to cross the Atlantic while in office
Death:	February 3, 1924
Age at Death:	67 years
Burial Place:	National Cathedral, Washington, D.C.

Fast Facts

Ellen Louise Axson Wilson

Birth:	May 15, 1860
Birthplace:	Savannah, Georgia
Parents:	Samuel and Margaret Hoyt Axson
Education:	Local schools and the Female Seminary in Rome, Georgia
Marriage:	To Woodrow Wilson, June 24, 1885
Children:	Margaret Woodrow Wilson (1886–1944)
	Jessie Woodrow Wilson (1887–1933)
	Eleanor Randolph Wilson (1889–1967)
Death:	August 6, 1914
Age at Death:	54 years
Burial Place:	Rome, Georgia

Edith Bolling Galt Wilson

Birth:	October 15, 1872
Birthplace:	Wytheville, Virginia
Parents:	William and Sallie White Bolling
Education:	Martha Washington College, Abingdon, Virginia
	Richmond Female Seminary, Virginia
Marriage:	To Norman Galt, April 30, 1896
	To Woodrow Wilson, December 18, 1915
Children:	None
Firsts:	First to stand beside her husband when he took the oath of office
	First to travel overseas as first lady
Death:	December 28, 1961
Age at Death:	89 years
Burial Place:	Washington, D.C.

Timeline

1856	1858	1870	1873	1875
Wilson is born in Staunton, Virginia	Wilson family moves to Augusta, Georgia	Family moves to Columbia, South Carolina	Wilson enrolls at Davidson College in North Carolina, attends for one school year	Enrolls at the College of New Jersey at Princeton

1890	1902	1910	1912	1913
Accepts teaching position at College of New Jersey, moves family to Princeton	Elected president of Princeton University	Elected governor of New Jersey	Elected president of the United States	Signs federal income tax law; proposes Federal Reserve System

1918	1919	1919	1920	1921
Announces the Armistice, ending fighting in World War I; sails to Europe for peace conference	Presents plan for League of Nations to Versailles peace conference; signs Versailles Treaty	Defends League of Nations on speaking tour; has a disabling stroke; awarded Nobel Peace Prize	Senate rejects Treaty of Versailles; Republican Warren G. Harding elected president	Wilson leaves office, retires to home in Washington, D.C.

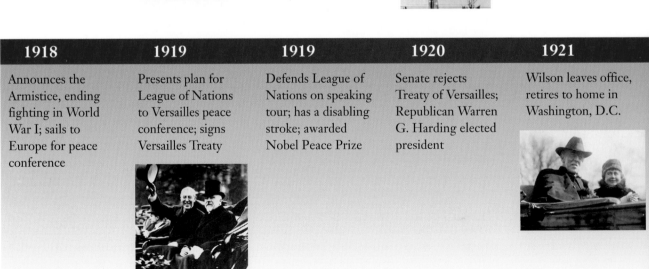

1879

Graduates from College of New Jersey; enters University of Virginia law school

1882

Begins brief law career in Atlanta, Georgia

1883

Begins graduate studies at Johns Hopkins University

1885

Marries Ellen Axson; publishes first book, *Congressional Government*; begins teaching career at Bryn Mawr College

1888

Becomes professor at Wesleyan University, Middletown, Connecticut

1914

World War I begins; U.S. occupies Veracruz, Mexico; Ellen Wilson dies

1915

Lusitania is sunk; U.S. remains neutral in war; Wilson marries Edith Bolling Galt

1916

Reelected president; sends troops into Mexico to pursue Pancho Villa; signs treaty for purchase of U.S. Virgin Islands from Denmark

1917

U.S. declares war on Germany; Wilson signs act creating the military draft

1918

Presents Fourteen Points in speech to Congress; supports women's suffrage amendment

1924

Wilson dies, February 3

Glossary

boss: a political leader who controls a political organization by rewarding party members with political jobs and other political favors

cabinet: the heads of federal government departments who meet to advise the president

direct primary: an election in which voters choose the parties' candidates for office

dyslexia: a learning disorder affecting the ability to read

electoral college: the group of electors representing the states that officially elects a president and vice president, as provided in the U.S. Constitution

initiative: a special vote in which citizens can establish a new law without the legislature's approval

monopoly: complete control of an industry by a single business corporation

pacifist: a person opposed to all wars

Parliament: the lawmaking body of the British government

ratify: to approve; the U.S. Senate must ratify treaties with other countries; the states must ratify proposed Constitutional amendments

recall: a special vote in which citizens can remove an elected official from office

referendum: a special vote in which citizens can repeal an unpopular law

reparations: payments that victorious nations impose on defeated nations as part of a treaty ending a war

reservations: restrictions or qualifications attached to an international agreement

self-determination: the right of a people to have a voice in creating a nation in which they will live

tariff: a tax on products imported into a country for sale

veto: refusal of an executive, such as a governor or president, to sign into law a bill passed by the legislature

Further Reading

★ ★ ★ ★

Brunelli, Carol, and Ann Gaines. *Woodrow Wilson: Our Twenty-Eighth President.* Chanhassen, MN: The Child's World. 2001.

Collins, David R. *Woodrow Wilson, 28th President of the United States.* Ada, OK: Garrett Educational Corporation, 1989.

Dommermuth-Costa, Carol. *Woodrow Wilson.* Minneapolis: Lerner Publishing Group, 2003.

Harmon, Daniel E. *Woodrow Wilson.* Broomall, PA: Mason Crest Publishers, 2003.

Holden, Henry M. *Woodrow Wilson.* Berkeley Heights, NJ: Enslow Publishers, 2003.

Sandak, Cass. *The Wilsons.* New York: Simon and Schuster, 1993.

MORE ADVANCED READING

Garraty, John A. *Woodrow Wilson.* New York: Harper and Row, 1956.

Heckscher, August. *Woodrow Wilson.* New York: Charles Scribner's Sons, 1991.

Levin, Phyllis Lee. *Edith and Woodrow.* New York: Scribner, 2001.

Macmillan, Margaret. *Paris 1919.* New York: Random House, 2002.

Smith, Gene. *When the Cheering Stopped: The Last Years of Woodrow Wilson.* New York: Time- Life Books, 1964.

Places to Visit

★ ★ ★ ★ ★

The New Jersey State House
Capitol Complex
Trenton, NJ 08625

Visit the state capitol building where Wilson
served as governor from 1911 to 1913.

Princeton University
Princeton, NJ 08544

See the campus where Wilson served as
university president from 1902 to 1910.

The White House
1600 Pennsylvania Avenue NW
Washington, DC 20500
Visitors' Office: (202) 456-7041

Tour the Executive Mansion where Wilson
and his family lived from 1913 to 1921.

**The Woodrow Wilson Presidential Library
   and Birthplace**
18-24 North Coalter Street
Staunton, VA 24402

See the house where Wilson was born in
1856.

The Woodrow Wilson House
2340 S Street NW
Washington, DC 20008

Tour exhibits in the house where Wilson
spent his last years.

Online Sites of Interest

★ **The American Presidency**

http://gi.grolier.com/presidents/

Supplies biographies of the presidents at different reading levels from materials in Scholastic/Grolier encyclopedias.

★ **Internet Public Library, Presidents of the United States (IPL POTUS)**

http://www.ipl.org/div/potus/wwilson.html

Excellent resource for personal, political, and historical materials about Woodrow Wilson. Includes links to other Internet sites.

★ **Presidents of Princeton**

http://www.princeton.edu/pr/facts/presidents/18.htm

Contains a detailed account of Wilson's years at Princeton as a student, teacher, and president.

★ **The White House**

http://www.whitehouse.gov/history/presidents/ww28.html

Provides information about the current president and vice president, a history of the Executive Mansion, virtual tours, biographies of U.S. presidents, and many other items of interest.

★ **Woodrow Wilson Birthplace**

http://woodrowwilson.org

Source of information about Wilson's birthplace, presidential library, and museum, and arrangements for tours.

★ **Woodrow Wilson House**

http://woodrowwilsonhouse.org

Has educational programs, newsletters, and calendars of events, based in the home where Wilson spent his last years in Washington, D.C.

Table of Presidents

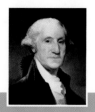   

	1. George Washington	**2. John Adams**	**3. Thomas Jefferson**	**4. James Madison**
Took office	Apr 30 1789	Mar 4 1797	Mar 4 1801	Mar 4 1809
Left office	Mar 3 1797	Mar 3 1801	Mar 3 1809	Mar 3 1817
Birthplace	Westmoreland Co, VA	Braintree, MA	Shadwell, VA	Port Conway, VA
Birth date	Feb 22 1732	Oct 20 1735	Apr 13 1743	Mar 16 1751
Death date	Dec 14 1799	July 4 1826	July 4 1826	June 28 1836

   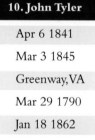 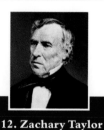

	9. William H. Harrison	**10. John Tyler**	**11. James K. Polk**	**12. Zachary Taylor**
Took office	Mar 4 1841	Apr 6 1841	Mar 4 1845	Mar 5 1849
Left office	**Apr 4 1841•**	Mar 3 1845	Mar 3 1849	**July 9 1850•**
Birthplace	Berkeley, VA	Greenway, VA	Mecklenburg Co, NC	Barboursville, VA
Birth date	Feb 9 1773	Mar 29 1790	Nov 2 1795	Nov 24 1784
Death date	Apr 4 1841	Jan 18 1862	June 15 1849	July 9 1850

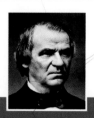 

	17. Andrew Johnson	**18. Ulysses S. Grant**	**19. Rutherford B. Hayes**	**20. James A. Garfield**
Took office	Apr 15 1865	Mar 4 1869	Mar 5 1877	Mar 4 1881
Left office	Mar 3 1869	Mar 3 1877	Mar 3 1881	**Sept 19 1881•**
Birthplace	Raleigh, NC	Point Pleasant, OH	Delaware, OH	Orange, OH
Birth date	Dec 29 1808	Apr 27 1822	Oct 4 1822	Nov 19 1831
Death date	July 31 1875	July 23 1885	Jan 17 1893	Sept 19 1881

	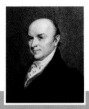		
5. James Monroe	**6. John Quincy Adams**	**7. Andrew Jackson**	**8. Martin Van Buren**
Mar 4 1817	Mar 4 1825	Mar 4 1829	Mar 4 1837
Mar 3 1825	Mar 3 1829	Mar 3 1837	Mar 3 1841
Westmoreland Co, VA	Braintree, MA	The Waxhaws, SC	Kinderhook, NY
Apr 28 1758	July 11 1767	Mar 15 1767	Dec 5 1782
July 4 1831	Feb 23 1848	June 8 1845	July 24 1862

13. Millard Fillmore	**14. Franklin Pierce**	**15. James Buchanan**	**16. Abraham Lincoln**
July 9 1850	Mar 4 1853	Mar 4 1857	Mar 4 1861
Mar 3 1853	Mar 3 1857	Mar 3 1861	**Apr 15 1865•**
Locke Township, NY	Hillsborough, NH	Cove Gap, PA	Hardin Co, KY
Jan 7 1800	Nov 23 1804	Apr 23 1791	Feb 12 1809
Mar 8 1874	Oct 8 1869	June 1 1868	Apr 15 1865

21. Chester A. Arthur	**22. Grover Cleveland**	**23. Benjamin Harrison**	**24. Grover Cleveland**
Sept 19 1881	Mar 4 1885	Mar 4 1889	Mar 4 1893
Mar 3 1885	Mar 3 1889	Mar 3 1893	Mar 3 1897
Fairfield, VT	Caldwell, NJ	North Bend, OH	Caldwell, NJ
Oct 5 1829	Mar 18 1837	Aug 20 1833	Mar 18 1837
Nov 18 1886	June 24 1908	Mar 13 1901	June 24 1908

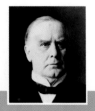

	25. William McKinley	26. Theodore Roosevelt	27. William H. Taft	28. Woodrow Wilson
Took office	Mar 4 1897	Sept 14 1901	Mar 4 1909	Mar 4 1913
Left office	Sept 14 1901•	Mar 3 1909	Mar 3 1913	Mar 3 1921
Birthplace	Niles, OH	New York, NY	Cincinnati, OH	Staunton, VA
Birth date	Jan 29 1843	Oct 27 1858	Sept 15 1857	Dec 28 1856
Death date	Sept 14 1901	Jan 6 1919	Mar 8 1930	Feb 3 1924

	33. Harry S. Truman	34. Dwight D. Eisenhower	35. John F. Kennedy	36. Lyndon B. Johnson
Took office	Apr 12 1945	Jan 20 1953	Jan 20 1961	Nov 22 1963
Left office	Jan 20 1953	Jan 20 1961	Nov 22 1963•	Jan 20 1969
Birthplace	Lamar, MO	Denison, TX	Brookline, MA	Johnson City, TX
Birth date	May 8 1884	Oct 14 1890	May 29 1917	Aug 27 1908
Death date	Dec 26 1972	Mar 28 1969	Nov 22 1963	Jan 22 1973

	41. George Bush	42. Bill Clinton	43. George W. Bush	
Took office	Jan 20 1989	Jan 20 1993	Jan 20 2001	
Left office	Jan 20 1993	Jan 20 2001	—	
Birthplace	Milton, MA	Hope, AR	New Haven, CT	
Birth date	June 12 1924	Aug 19 1946	July 6 1946	
Death date	—	—	—	

29. Warren G. Harding	30. Calvin Coolidge	31. Herbert Hoover	32. Franklin D. Roosevelt
Mar 4 1921	Aug 2 1923	Mar 4 1929	Mar 4 1933
Aug 2 1923•	Mar 3 1929	Mar 3 1933	**Apr 12 1945•**
Blooming Grove, OH	Plymouth, VT	West Branch, IA	Hyde Park, NY
Nov 21 1865	July 4 1872	Aug 10 1874	Jan 30 1882
Aug 2 1923	Jan 5 1933	Oct 20 1964	Apr 12 1945

37. Richard M. Nixon	38. Gerald R. Ford	39. Jimmy Carter	40. Ronald Reagan
Jan 20 1969	Aug 9 1974	Jan 20 1977	Jan 20 1981
Aug 9 1974★	Jan 20 1977	Jan 20 1981	Jan 20 1989
Yorba Linda, CA	Omaha, NE	Plains, GA	Tampico, IL
Jan 9 1913	July 14 1913	Oct 1 1924	Feb 6 1911
Apr 22 1994	—	—	June 5 2004

• Indicates the president died while in office.

★ Richard Nixon resigned before his term expired.

Index

About the Author

Barbara Silberdick Feinberg graduated with honors from Wellesley College where she was elected to Phi Beta Kappa and received the Woodrow Wilson Prize for an Essay in Modern Politics. She holds a Ph.D. in political science from Yale University. Among her more recent works are *Watergate: Scandal in the White House*; *American Political Scandals Past and Present*; *The National Government*; *State Governments*; *Local Governments*; *Words in the News: A Student's Dictionary of American Government and Politics*; *Harry S Truman*; *John Marshall: The Great Chief Justice*; *Electing the President; The Cabinet*; *Hiroshima and Nagasaki*; *Black Tuesday: The Stock Market Crash of 1929*; *Term Limits for Congress*; *The Constitutional Amendments*; *Next in Line: The American Vice Presidency*; *Patricia Ryan Nixon*; *Elizabeth Wallace Truman*; *Edith Kermit Carow Roosevelt*; *America's First Ladies: Changing Expectations*; *General Douglas MacArthur: An American Hero*; *The Dictionary of the U.S. Constitution*; *The Changing White House*; *Abraham Lincoln and the Gettysburg Address*; *Four Score and More*; *The Articles of Confederation: The First Constitution of the United States*; *John McCain: Serving His Country*; *Joseph I. Lieberman: Keeping the Faith*; *Eleanor Roosevelt: A Very Special First Lady*; *John Adams*; and *Woodrow Wilson*. She has also written *Marx and Marxism*; *The Constitution: Yesterday, Today, and Tomorrow*; and *Franklin Roosevelt, Gallant President* and has contributed entries to *The Young Reader's Companion to American History*.

Mrs. Feinberg is a native New Yorker and the mother of two sons, Jeremy and Douglas.